CONSERVATORY CANADA™

THEORY & HISTORY SYLLABUS 2014 EDITION
Effective September 2014

This Syllabus is essentially a reproduction of the 1999 edition, with updated Theory 4 requirements from 2007, and updated History 5, 6, and 7 repertoire lists from 2011. Also included are updates in the Bibliography, recommended texts, and various small changes within the *General Information & Regulations.*

Editor:

Peter J. Clements, Director of Theoretical Studies, Conservatory Canada

Editorial Committee:

Karin Andrews
Jan Danowski
Patricia Frelich
Sean Kim
Kelly Matthews
Derek Oger
Darlene Chepil Reid

1999 Syllabus Committee:

Dorothy Buckley
John Burge
Patricia Mitsis
Patricia Stretch
Hugheen Ferguson
David Greenslade

Welcome to Conservatory Canada

The two founding institutions of Conservatory Canada bring the past and the future together, creating a new, nation-wide organization out of two eminent regional institutes.

Western Ontario Conservatory of Music in London, Ontario was established in 1891 and incorporated in 1934. Throughout the years it has maintained a teaching facility, and began offering province-wide examinations in the late 1930's. This was later expanded to serve Atlantic Canada.

Music teachers and university administrators in the provinces of Alberta, Saskatchewan and Manitoba formed The Joint Board of Music for Western Canada in 1934. Soon renamed The Western Board of Music, it developed a comprehensive examination system to serve the three Prairie provinces, and in recent decades expanded into British Columbia.

In September 1997, both Western Ontario Conservatory and The Western Board merged to create Conservatory Canada. Conservatory Canada's office is now located in London, Ontario.

Within and outside the regular examination system, each founding institution has sought to provide teachers and students with varied, innovative programs and features. Oral questions, supplementary pieces, mini-lessons, recital assessments and teacher development assessments have all been carried over into the new syllabi and program offerings of Conservatory Canada.

Previous credits earned with either Western Ontario Conservatory or The Western Board are automatically retained, and are now portable throughout Canada. Production and revision of syllabi, repertoire books and other support materials is an ongoing process.

Conservatory Canada offers the best of two worlds, the new and the old: a new national vision for the 21st century, steeped in the traditions of two venerable Canadian examination systems. We welcome the opportunity to serve Canadian musicians, both young and old, amateur and professional, from coast to coast.

Contents

GENERAL INFORMATION & REGULATIONS

This Syllabus contains regulations and requirements for **Theory** examinations for Theory 1 to Theory 7 and **History** examinations for History 5 to History 7.

GENERAL INFORMATION

Subjects

Examinations are offered in the following subject areas:

Practical

Piano	Violin	Trumpet	Flute
Organ (pipe)	Viola	French Horn	Clarinet
	Violoncello	Trombone	Saxophone
Guitar	Voice	Tuba	Teacher Development

Written

Theory (Rudiments)	Music History	Piano Pedagogy
Theory (Harmony)	Theory (Form & Analysis)	

Sessions

Practical Examinations

The Conservatory conducts three practical examination sessions during each academic year. These examinations include most instruments and voice, and are held at centres throughout Canada (new centres may be established by arrangement with the Conservatory):

1. WINTER SESSION: the first three weeks in February
(application deadline is normally in mid-November)
2. SPRING SESSION: the entire month of June
(application deadline is normally in mid-March)
3. SUMMER SESSION: the second and third weeks of August
(application deadline is normally in mid-June)

Applicants should consult the Conservatory Canada website for the deadline date of the specific session for which they wish to apply.

The Conservatory will make every effort to schedule practical examinations around legitimate events, such as school trips or school examinations, provided notice is given IN WRITING AT THE TIME OF APPLICATION. However, because of constraints in reserving facilities and Examiners, *this cannot be guaranteed, and by submitting an application, the candidate agrees to appear for the examination as scheduled.* Candidates entering the June examinations must understand that it is not always possible to schedule music examinations around school examinations.

Candidates will be given at least two weeks notice of the date, time and place of the practical examination. *Under no circumstances are candidates or their teachers permitted to change dates or times of the scheduled examination.* Examiners are instructed not to make schedule changes unless such changes have been authorized by the Office of the Registrar.

Written Examinations

The Conservatory conducts three written examination sessions during each academic year throughout Canada (new centres may be established by arrangement with the Conservatory):

1. WINTER SESSION: second Saturday in January
    (application deadline is normally early in mid-November)

2. SPRING SESSION: second Saturday in May
    (application deadline is normally in mid-March)

3. SUMMER SESSION: second Saturday in August
    (application deadline is normally in mid-June)

Applicants should consult the Conservatory Canada website for the exam and deadline date for the specific session for which they wish to apply.

Written examinations are scheduled to begin at 9am on the set exam date.

Candidates applying to write two examinations in the same session will have one exam scheduled at 9am, and the second exam scheduled at 1pm.

Applications

All applications must be submitted on the Student Portal at
www.ccexaminations.ca.

Applications submitted after the deadline date will be subject to a $30 late fee.

Centres

Practical

Practical examinations are conducted by fully qualified Examiners appointed by the Conservatory in those centres where the number of applicants is deemed sufficient. The Conservatory reserves the right to defer examinations until a later session in any centre where the enrollment does not warrant the visit of an Examiner, or to require the candidate to travel to the nearest viable centre. The best facilities available will be provided for examinations, in centres as close as possible to the candidate's hometown. Candidates should plan to arrive at least 15 minutes before the examination is scheduled to begin.

Written

Written examinations are held in centres where there are a minimum of six candidates.

When there are fewer than six candidates registered in a given centre, then the candidate will be given the option of travelling to the nearest viable examination centre, or of making special arrangements through the Conservatory. Regardless of which option is followed, all examinations must be written on the designated exam day. In the case of special arrangements, candidates (or their teacher) will be asked to find a suitable place to write the examination, such as a school or church, and to provide their own Presiding Officer to supervise the examination. The Presiding Officer will be a responsible adult, but cannot be the music teacher or parents of the candidate. Please consult the Conservatory for further details.

Payment of Fees

The appropriate fee must be paid by Visa or MasterCard when the online application form is completed on the Student Portal.

Re-evaluation of Written Papers

It is the policy of the Conservatory that when an examination paper contains a question or musical example that is inaccurate or that falls outside syllabus requirements, all candidates will automatically be given full credit for that question or portion of it. However, candidates who feel that, for other reasons, they have reason to question the mark they received on the examination may apply to have their paper re-read. Request for a re-read must be made in writing to the Office of the Registrar within 30 days from the date the marks were issued. The request must include the complete paper without alterations and the appropriate fee. Should the re-read show that there was fault on the part of the examiner or the Conservatory, the fee will be refunded in full. We regret that we are unable to respond to verbal requests concerning the reported mark.

Appeals

Queries or appeals concerning the examination procedure must be filed in writing with the Office of the Registrar within 10 days of the completion of the examination.

Cancellations

Notice of withdrawal, for any reason, must be submitted in writing to the Office of the Registrar. Consult the Conservatory Canada website for refund policy regarding cancellations by the candidate before the scheduled date of the examination. No refund will be considered for notice of cancellation, for whatever reason, received after the scheduled date of the examination.

Marking Standards

The Conservatory's standard of marking, in Grades 1-10 is as follows:

First-Class Honours with Distinction	90-100 marks
First-Class Honours	80-89 marks
Honours	70-79 marks
Pass	60-69 marks
Insufficient to Pass	Below 60 marks

Results and Notices

All examination notices, results and certificates are posted on the Student Portal. Under no condition will examination results be released verbally, either in person or by telephone. Because examination marks are confidential to the teacher and candidate, results CANNOT be released to any other person.

Transfer Credits

Transfer credit is not possible for practical subjects. However, candidates who have completed successfully equivalent examinations in Theory and History courses at recognized conservatories and/or universities may apply in writing for consideration for transfer credit. If approved, the transfer credit can be used to satisfy the co-requisite requirement for the awarding of a practical certificate. The following regulations will apply:

1) To apply for a transcript evaluation with a view to obtaining transfer credit, candidates must:

    a. Submit a letter of application, with the appropriate fee, to the Office of the Registrar.

    b. Arrange to have an official transcript (or letter) sent by the issuing institution **directly** to the Office of the Registrar. No application for transfer credit will be considered until the official transcript is received. Transcripts sent by the candidate are NOT acceptable.

2) Transfer credit will NOT be considered for co-requisite courses complete more than TEN years before the scheduled date of the practical examination session.

Medals for Excellence

A Medal for Excellence will be awarded to the candidate who receives the highest mark (minimum mark of 85%) in each grade for each province for the academic year. To be eligible, candidates must complete the examination in one sitting, and also must have completed successfully all of the prescribed Theory and History co-requisites, if appropriate. Candidates who are considered to be professional musicians, and candidates who take partial or supplemental examinations are NOT eligible for medals.

Scholarships and Awards

Endowed Scholarships

The annual interest earned by the Conservatory's Scholarship Endowment Fund supports over 30 scholarships each year. Scholarships range from $300 to $1000 and must be used for music tuition with any teacher anywhere in Canada. Scholarships are awarded based on examination results, and most scholarships are available to all examination candidates at any centre. The Scholarship Endowment Funds are held in trust and managed by the London Community Foundation and the University of Alberta. Please contact the Conservatory office for a list of current scholarships and conditions.

Prizes and Awards

From time to time, donations are received to be given as occasional prizes and awards (usually under $300). These will be awarded as stipulated by the donor and will be presented directly to the student.

Certificates

Certificates are awarded for all practical, theory and history examinations upon the successful completion of all requirements. For practical examinations in Grades 5 to 10, certificates will be issued subject to the completion of theory/history co-requisite requirements listed for each grade.

Academic Credits

Conservatory Canada examination candidates may be eligible for Secondary School curriculum credits according to the requirements as outlined by the various provincial Ministries of Education.

Candidates are strongly advised to consult with their own school officials in order to determine their eligibility in their province of residence.

Visually-Impaired or Physically-Challenged Candidates

Special provisions can be made for visually-impaired or physically-challenged candidates. For details, please contact the Office of the Registrar *before the closing date for applications.*

Theory & History Co-requisites For Practical Certificates (Grades 1-10)

Theoretical subjects are required for practical Certificates for all instruments and voice beyond Grade 4. Certificates are issued only when the required Theory and/or History co-requisites are completed. Candidates must complete their written co-requisites within 5 years of the practical examination.

Because the requirements of this Syllabus have been carefully designed as a progressively graded study, candidates are encouraged to take each written examination in sequence. Nevertheless, candidates for Theory examinations may choose to enter the program at any grade level. Therefore, the successful completion of a particular grade level will be considered as having fulfilled all co-requisites at the lower levels. (For example, candidates who complete Theory 3 as their first examination, will have fulfilled the lower level co-requisites required for the Practical Certificate in Grades 5, 6, and 7).

However, this does NOT apply to candidates in History who must successfully complete each grade of History.

THEORY & HISTORY CO-REQISITES FOR PRACTICAL CERTIFICATES

Practical Grade	Theory and/or History Requirements
1	No requirement
2	No requirement
3	No requirement
4	No requirement
5	Theory 1
6	Theory 2
7	Theory 3
8	Theory 4
9	Theory 5 History 5 OR History 6 (candidates choice)
10	Theory 6 History 5 or History 6
Associate (Performer)	Theory 7a (Harmony/Counterpoint) Theory 7b (Form & Analysis) History 7
Associate (Teacher)	Theory 7a (Harmony/Counterpoint) Theory 7b (Form & Analysis) History 7 Piano Pedagogy

INSTRUCTIONS FOR WRITTEN EXAMINATIONS

1. Textbooks, workbooks and student notes are not permitted in the examination room. Candidates need provide only a pencil or pen and eraser.

2. Only the candidates and the presiding officer are permitted in the examination room.

3. Candidates may leave the room when they have finished the examination. However, candidates will not be permitted to re-enter the room once they have left.

4. All questions must be answered in the appropriate place on the examination paper. Additional paper and manuscript paper will be provided for rough work.

5. Candidates should consult their 'notice of examination' slip for their exam date and time. Candidates should arrive at the examination centre at least 15 minutes before the examination is scheduled to begin.

6. It is recommended that Theory candidates prepare for the examination by checking completed exercises by playing them at the keyboard. This will strengthen the relationship between what you have written and how it sounds and will also serve to improve your aural skills.

7. Accurate, neat musical notation is expected. Sloppy or ambiguous notation cannot be given full credit and will be reflected in the marking.

8. History candidates should write or print neatly and clearly. Marks will be deducted for incorrect spelling of composers' names, titles of works, and musical terms. Though the use of proper grammar is expected, marks will be deducted only if poor grammar obscures the clarity of the answer.

9. For the study of Theory and History, no one text is in itself complete. Though it is not unusual to encounter discrepancies among different sources, candidates are encouraged to consult a variety of sources. Musical terminology can also differ, so for the purposes of these examinations, terminology found in any of the suggested text books is acceptable.

10. Because music is a highly-structured combination of sounds, created by composers working in different periods and musical styles, it is essential that Theory and History students become familiar with musical scores and recordings of works by composers who represent the period and compositional style being studied. Particular works are mentioned under particular grades in the Syllabus.

11. History candidates may write their answers in either English or French.

12. All examination results will be posted on the Student Portal at www.ccexaminations.ca.

13. Copies of past examination papers may be purchased online, or by calling the Conservatory Canada office.

14. In preparation for the examination, students may submit completed papers to the Conservatory for written comment and critique. Please contact the Conservatory Office for further details and fees.

Candidates are expected to know all of the current regulations and requirements for the examinations as outlined in this Syllabus. No allowance can be made for candidates who misread or fail to follow any of the regulations and/or requirements for the examination.

THEORY 1

ONE PAPER: **Time: 1-½ Hours**

RECOMMENDED TEXT   Fielder, Steven & Cook, D.F. ***Conservatory Canada Theory for Students, Book 1*** (Novus Via Music/Hal Leonard 2014)

CO-REQUISITE   Successful complete of Theory 1 is required to obtain a certificate for the Grade 5 Practical Examination.

Note: For examination purposes, musical terminology will be as used in the Recommended Text.

REQUIREMENTS

Keys required for this examination:

Major	Up to and including FOUR sharps and FOUR flats
Minor	Up to and including FOUR sharps and FOUR flats

1. Notation
•Treble and bass clefs •Names of notes (not more than TWO leger lines above or below the staff) •Accidentals – sharp, flat, and natural (NO double sharps or double flats) •Whole tones, semitones (chromatic and diatonic) •Stem directions •Accurate placing of clefs and accidentals •Function of barlines in cancelling accidentals (*Marks will be deducted for redundant and unnecessary accidentals. The ambiguity of accidentals enclosed within a bracket (#) is to be avoided.*)

2. Rhythm
•Time values of notes and rests (and their relative values) from whole to 16th •Triplet eighth notes •Adding time signatures, barlines, notes and rests in SIMPLE TIME ONLY •Proper grouping of notes and rests.

3. Scales

- Major scales
- Minor scales (natural, harmonic, and melodic forms)
- Beginning on the tonic only
- To be written within a given time signature (Simple time only), in note values as requested, and completing the *final bar only* with rests, if necessary.
- Mark semitones with a slur
- Identify tonic and dominant notes in the scale

4. Intervals

- Identify or write major, minor, and perfect intervals
- Above a given note
- Harmonic and melodic forms
- Simple intervals only

5. Triads

- Identify or write tonic, dominant, and sub-dominant triads only
- In major AND minor keys
- Root position only
- Close position only
- Raised leading-notes required in minor keys

6. Transposition

- Identify the key of a given melody (the key signature will be given)
- Major keys ONLY
- Transpose up and down ONE octave. May be in the same clef, or to/from treble or bass clef

7. Simple Analysis

- Analysis of a short passage in piano score
- Identify such details as the composer, title, key, time signature, musical terms and signs, intervals, triads

8. Melody Writing
•Write a two-bar phrase to complete a given two-bar melody (no anacrusis) •The added phrase must be musically designed and must end on the tonic •The melody will be limited to a range of five notes

9. Terms
As given in Fielder and Cook, ***Conservatory Canada Theory for Students, Book 1***

THEORY 2

ONE PAPER:	**Time: 2 Hours**
RECOMMENDED TEXT	Fielder, Steven & Cook, D.F. *Conservatory Canada Theory for Students, Book 2* (Novus Via Music/Hal Leonard 2014)
CO-REQUISITE	Successful complete of Theory 2 is required to obtain a certificate for the Grade 6 Practical Examination.

Note: For examination purposes, musical terminology will be as used in the Recommended Text.

REQUIREMENTS

Keys required for this examination:

Major	ALL keys
Minor	ALL keys

1. Notation
•Treble and bass clefs •Names of notes (not more than THREE leger lines above or below the staff) •Accidentals – sharp, flat, natural, double sharp, double flat •Whole tones, semitones (chromatic and diatonic) •Stem directions •Accurate placing of clefs and accidentals •Function of barlines in cancelling accidentals (*Marks will be deducted for redundant and unnecessary accidentals. The ambiguity of accidentals enclosed within a bracket (#) is to be avoided.*)

2. Rhythm
•Time values of notes and rests (and their relative values) from whole to 32nd •Triplet quarter, eighth, and sixteenth notes •Duplet eighth and sixteenth notes •Adding time signatures, barlines, notes and rests in Simple AND compound time •Proper grouping of notes and rests.

3. Scales

- Major scales
- Minor scales (natural, harmonic, and melodic forms)
- Beginning on the tonic only
- To be written within a given time signature (simple time only), in note values as requested, and completing the *final bar only* with rests, if necessary.
- Mark semitones with a slur
- Identify technical names (*i.e.* tonic, mediant, etc.) for ALL degrees of the scale

4. Intervals

- Identify or write major, minor, perfect, augmented and diminished intervals
- Above a given note
- Harmonic and melodic forms
- Simple intervals only

5. Triads/Chords

- Identify or write ALL major and minor 4-note chords
- Doubling will be specified
- Tonic, dominant, and sub-dominant 3-note triads only
- In major AND minor keys
- Root position and 1st and 2nd inversions
- Close AND open position

6. Cadences

- Perfect and Plagal cadences only in root position
- Identify only by name and chord symbol (candidates are NOT required to write cadences)
- In keyboard style only

7. Transposition

- Identify the key of a given melody (the key signature may or may NOT be given)
- Major keys ONLY
- Transpose up and down ANY interval

8. Simple Analysis
•Analysis of a short passage in piano score •Identify such details as the composer, title, key, time signature, musical terms and signs, intervals, triads, cadences

9. Melody Writing
•Write a two-bar phrase to complete a given two-bar melody (may include an anacrusis) •The added phrase must be musically designed and must end on a note of the tonic triad •The given phrase will be within the range of one octave

10. Terms
As given in Fielder and Cook, *Conservatory Canada Theory for Students, Book 2*

THEORY 3

ONE PAPER:	**Time: 2 Hours**
RECOMMENDED TEXT	Cook, D.F. ***Conservatory Canada Theory for Students, Book 3*** (Novus Via Music/Hal Leonard 2014)
CO-REQUISITE	Successful complete of Theory 3 is required to obtain a certificate for the Grade 7 Practical Examination.

Note: For examination purposes, musical terminology will be as used in the Recommended Text.

REQUIREMENTS

Candidates must know all requirements for Theory 1 and Theory 2, AND additional requirements as follows:

Keys required for this examination

Major	ALL keys
Minor	ALL keys

1. Notation
•Treble, bass, AND C-clefs •Names of notes (not more than FOUR leger lines above or below the staff) •ALL Accidentals – sharp, flat, natural, double sharp, double flat •Whole tones, semitones (chromatic and diatonic) •Stem directions •Accurate placing of clefs and accidentals •Function of barlines in cancelling accidentals (*Marks will be deducted for redundant and unnecessary accidentals. The ambiguity of accidentals enclosed within a bracket (#) is to be avoided.*)

2. Rhythm
•Time values of notes and rests (and their relative values) from whole to 32nd •Triplet quarter, eighth, and sixteenth notes •Duplet eighth and sixteenth notes •Adding time signatures, barlines, notes and rests in Simple, Compound, AND Irregular (5/4, 5/8, 7/4, 7/8) time signatures •Proper grouping of notes and rests.

3. Scales
•Major scales •Minor scales (natural, harmonic, and melodic forms) •Beginning on ANY degree of the scale •To be written within a given time signature (Simple and Compound time), in note values as requested, and completing the *final bar only* with rests, if necessary. •Mark semitones with a slur, and, for harmonic minor, identify the augmented 2nd •Identify technical names (*i.e.* tonic, mediant, etc.) for ALL degrees of the scale •Whole Tone Scale beginning on C or F

4. Intervals
•Identify or write major, minor, perfect, augmented and diminished intervals •Above and below a given note •Harmonic and melodic forms •Simple AND compound intervals •Inversions of simple intervals •Enharmonic equivalents

5. Triads/Chords
Identify or write primary and secondary 4-note chords (doubling will be specified) •Major, Minor, Augmented, and Diminished •Dominant 7th Chords •In ALL major and minor keys •Root position, and all inversions •Close AND open position •Keyboard and SATB style •Identify using chord symbols and figures

6. Cadences
To identify only •Perfect, Plagal, and Imperfect two-chord cadences •Root position ONLY •Identify only by name and chord symbol •In keyboard or SATB style

7. Transposition
•Identify the key of a given passage (the key signature may or may NOT be given) •In any major or minor key •Transpose up and down ANY interval

8. Open Score
•Transcribe a piano passage into open score •Modern choral score only

9. Ornaments
To realize ornaments as follows •appoggiatura •acciaccatura (grace note) •upper and lower mordent

10. Simple Analysis

- Analysis of a short passage in piano score
- Identify such details as the composer, title, key, time signature, musical terms and signs, intervals, triads, cadences

11. Melody Writing

- Write a four-bar phrase to complete a given four-bar melody (may include an anacrusis)
- The added phrase must be musically designed and must end on a note of the tonic triad
- The range of the melody may exceed one octave, and may move above and/or below the tonic

10. Terms

As given in Cook, **_Conservatory Canada Theory for Students, Book 3_**

THEORY 4

ONE PAPER:	**Time: 2 Hours**
RECOMMENDED TEXT	Cook, D.F. *Conservatory Canada Theory for Students, Book 4* (Novus Via Music/Hal Leonard 2014)
CO-REQUISITE	Successful completion of Theory 4 is required to obtain a certificate for the Grade 8 Practical Examination.

Note: For examination purposes, musical terminology will be as used in the Recommended Text.

REQUIREMENTS

Candidates must know all requirements up to and including Theory 3 AND additional requirements as follows:

Keys required for this examination

Major	ALL keys
Minor	ALL keys

---

1. Non-Diatonic Scales

To identify or write **using simple and compound (but not irregular) time signatures**
•Whole Tone Scale beginning on **ANY note, without key signatures**
To identify or write the following scales, using whole notes. Time signature and rhythm are not required:
•Chromatic Scale (**harmonic form only**) beginning on ANY note; **with or without key signature**
•Pentatonic Scale, beginning on **ANY note of the C pentatonic or F# pentatonic scale**
•Blues Scale **on C**, beginning on **ANY note, without key signature**

All scales may be ascending or descending or both. The starting note should be repeated at the octave. Candidates will not be required to identify non-diatonic scales in analysis excerpts.

2. Modes
To identify or write using white keys only (time signature and rhythm are not required) the following modes (authentic forms only): **Dorian, Phrygian, Lydian, Mixolydian, Aeolian, Locrian, and Ionian.** **Candidates will not be required to identify modes in analysis excerpts.   Transposed modes are NOT required.**

3. Figured Bass
(a)**To IDENTIFY any major, minor, augmented, or diminished chord, and all inversions, or Dominant 7th chords in root position or 1st inversion only, individually or in a progression.   Non-chord tones may be present.** (b)To **REALIZE** chords individually or in progression (**maximum 16 chords), without non-chord tones.** •in Major AND minor keys •using Major and minor chords only, root position and 1st inversion **only, and the tonic cadential 6/4 chord** •Dominant 7ths root position and 1st inversion **only** •The first chord will be realized

4. Cadences & Simple Chord Progression
To harmonize a four-chord progression **ABOVE a given bass only.** Begin with the tonic chord and continue with: i)A preparatory chord **in major keys: using ii, ii6, IV, IV6 or I6/4** **in minor keys: using iv, iv6 or i6/4** ii) a Perfect or **Interrupted cadence only** •Major AND minor keys •Using V or V7 •Identify cadences by name •Identify all chords using either Roman symbols and figures, or chord symbols (C+, G7 etc.) •In SATB style only, following the accepted rules of spacing and voice leading

5. Transposition
•Identify the key of a given melody (the key signature may or may not be given) •In any major or minor key •Transpose a simple passage (in piano or open vocal score) up or down any interval. •Transcribe a simple melodic line **given in concert pitch,** for the following transposing instruments: clarinet in B♭, clarinet in A, trumpet in B♭, trumpet in D, Horn in F **Viola is excluded**

6. Open Score
•Transcribe a passage from **four-part** short (keyboard) score into open score or *vice versa* using: •**Open Modern Vocal** score •**Open** String Quartet score

7. Melody Writing
•Write a four-bar phrase to complete a given four-bar melody (may include an anacrusis) •The added phrase must be musically designed and must end on a note of the tonic triad •The range of the melody may exceed one octave, and may move above and/or below the tonic •Identify by name and chord symbols the probable cadences implied at the end of each phrase.

8. Harmonic Analysis (using either Roman numerals & figures, or chord symbols (C+, G7 etc.)
To provide a harmonic analysis of a brief excerpt in short score, keyboard or chorale style (NO modulation) as follows: •Identify the key •**Use either Roman numerals with figures as necessary, or chord symbols (C+, G7 etc.)** •**Major and minor chords only, in root position and 1st inversion, and the cadential 6/4** •**Dominant 7th chord in root position and 1st inversion** •**Non-chord tones** are to be circled and labelled •Label all cadences

9. Non-chord (Unessential Tones)

- To identify **and/or** write:
- unaccented passing notes (**in all voices**)
- accented passing notes (**in SAT only**)
- unaccented upper and **lower** auxiliary notes (**in all voices**)
- **accented upper** and **lower** auxiliary notes (**in SAT only**)
- appoggiatura (**in SAT only**)
- anticipation notes (**in SAT only**)

THEORY 5

ONE PAPER: **Time: 3 Hours**

RECOMMENDED TEXTS

No one text is complete insofar as these requirements are concerned and, though discrepancies between sources are not unusual, candidates are encouraged to consult a variety of sources. A selective list of theory resource books may be found under the Bibliography section at the end of this syllabus. However, though candidates may choose any text book(s) the following are recommended.

Aldwell, Schachter & Cadwaller, **Harmony & Voice Leading, 4th edition.** (Schirmer / Cengage Learning, 2011) Workbook, CD of musical examples, and supporting internet resources are available.

Schubert and Neidhofer, **Baroque Counterpoint.** (Pearson/ Prentice Hall 2006)

CO-REQUISITE

Successful completion of Theory 5 is required to obtain a certificate for the Grade 9 Practical Examination.

Note: Musical terminology as used in either of the recommended texts is acceptable for examination purposes.

REQUIREMENTS

Candidates must know all requirements for all grades up to and including Theory 4, AND additional requirements as follows

Keys required for this examination

Major	ALL keys
Minor	ALL keys

Candidates are expected to be familiar with the use of the following:

Major and Minor Chords (root position and inversions)
Dominant 7th chords (root position and inversions) with resolutions
Cadential 6/4 chords
Secondary Dominants, V/V and V7/V only (root position and inversions)

Non-chord Tones
    • passing notes (accented and unaccented)
    • auxiliary (neighbour) notes
    • appoggiatura
    • anticipation notes
    • escape tones

Modulation to Dominant only

1. Harmony (Chorale Style)
Provide four-part harmony for SATB in Baroque chorale style, for a given melody or bass (figured or unfigured), observing the accepted rules of voice leading.   • Major keys only   • May modulate to the dominant   • Use non-chord tones   • Harmonic analysis using chord symbols and figures may be required

2. Harmony (Keyboard Style)
Harmonize a given melody and/or bass in keyboard style (approximately 8 bars in length)   • Major keys only   • May modulate to the dominant   • A harmonic rhythm that follows, in general, two chords per bar   • Rhythmic and melodic interest, flow and unity   • Harmonic analysis using chord symbols and figures may be required   • The first bar will be given complete to indicate the style

3. Counterpoint
Add a second part above or below a given melody in 18th-century counterpoint (approximately 8 bars in length)   • Give chordal analysis of implied harmony   • Use rhythmic and motivic ideas derived from the example(s) given on the question paper

4. Analysis
Analysis of a short passage in piano or SATB score in Binary or Rounded Binary form • Identify key • Mark phrases and cadences • Identify main key centres, points of modulation, and structural divisions • Harmonic analysis using chord symbols and figures • Circle and label non-harmonic tones

THEORY 6

ONE PAPER: **Time: 3 Hours**

RECOMMENDED TEXTS

No one text is complete insofar as these requirements are concerned and, though discrepancies between sources are not unusual, candidates are encouraged to consult a variety of sources. A selective list of theory resource books may be found under the Bibliography section at the end of this syllabus. However, though candidates may choose any text book(s) the following are recommended.

Aldwell, Schachter & Cadwaller, **Harmony & Voice Leading, 4th edition.** (Schirmer / Cengage Learning, 2011) Workbook, CD of musical examples, and supporting internet resources are available.

Schubert and Neidhofer, **Baroque Counterpoint.** (Pearson/ Prentice Hall 2006)

CO-REQUISITE

Successful completion of Theory 6 is required to obtain a certificate for the Grade 10 Practical Examination.

Note: Musical terminology as used in either of the recommended texts is acceptable for examination purposes.

REQUIREMENTS

Candidates must know all requirements for all grades up to and including Theory 5, AND additional requirements as follows

Keys required for this examination

Major	ALL keys
Minor	ALL keys

Candidates are expected to be familiar with the use of the following:

| Major, Minor, Diminished Chords (root position and inversions) |
| Dominant 9th and 13th chords (root position only) |
| Diatonic 7th chords (root position and inversions) |
| Secondary (Applied) Dominants (root position and inversions) |
| Secondary (Applied) Diminished 7th of V (root position and inversions) |
| Modulation to closely related keys |
| Non-chord Tones
• passing notes (accented and unaccented)
• auxiliary (neighbour) notes
• appoggiatura
• anticipation notes
• escape tones
• suspensions |

| **1. Harmony (Chorale Style)** |
| Provide four-part harmony for SATB in Baroque chorale style, for a given melody or bass (figured or unfigured), observing the accepted rules of voice leading.
• Major and minor keys
• Modulation to closely related keys
• Non-chord tones
• Harmonic analysis using chord symbols and figures may be required |

| **2. Harmony (Keyboard Style)** |
| Harmonize a given melody and/or bass in keyboard style (approximately 8-12 bars in length)
• Major and minor keys
• The first bar will be given complete to indicate the style and period (*i.e.* Baroque, Classical, or Romantic)
• Modulation to closely related keys
• Rhythmic and melodic interest, flow and unity
• Harmonic analysis using chord symbols and figures may be required |

3. Counterpoint
Add a second part above or below a given melody in 18th-century counterpoint (approximately 8-12 bars in length) • Give chordal analysis of implied harmony • Use rhythmic and motivic ideas derived from the example(s) given on the question paper

4. Analysis
Analysis of a short passage in piano or SATB score in Binary, Rounded Binary, or Ternary form • Identify key • Trace thematic development • Mark phrases and cadences • Identify main key centres, points of modulation, and structural divisions • Harmonic analysis using chord symbols and figures • All non-chord tones to be circled and labelled

THEORY 7(A)

HARMONY & COUNTERPOINT

(Associate Diploma)

ONE PAPER: **Time: 3 Hours**

RECOMMENDED TEXTS

No one text is complete insofar as these requirements are concerned and, though discrepancies between sources are not unusual, candidates are encouraged to consult a variety of sources. A selective list of theory resource books may be found under the Bibliography section at the end of this syllabus. However, though candidates may choose any text book(s) the following are recommended.

Aldwell, Schachter & Cadwaller, **Harmony & Voice Leading, 4th edition.** (Schirmer / Cengage Learning, 2011) Workbook, CD of musical examples, and supporting internet resources are available.

Schubert and Neidhofer, **Baroque Counterpoint.** (Pearson/ Prentice Hall 2006)

CO-REQUISITE

Successful completion of Theory 7(A) is required to obtain the ASSOCIATE DIPLOMA.

Note: Musical terminology as used in either of the recommended texts is acceptable for examination purposes.

REQUIREMENTS

Candidates must know all requirements for all grades up to and including Theory 6, AND additional requirements as follows

Keys required for this examination

Major	ALL keys
Minor	ALL keys

Candidates are expected to be familiar with the use of the following:

Major, Minor, Augmented, Diminished Chords (root position and inversions)
Advanced use of Secondary (Applied) Dominant chords (root position and inversions
Advanced use of Secondary (Applied) Diminished 7th of V (root position and inversions)

Altered Chords
    • Neapolitan 6th chord
    • Augmented 6th chords

All Non-chord tones
Modulation to any key

1. Harmony (Chorale Style)
Harmonize for SATB in chorale style, a melody and/or bass (figured or unfigured), observing the accepted rules of voice leading, and using • Modulation to any key • Neapolitan chords • Augmented 6th chords • Suspensions, and non-harmonic notes • The question will provide a portion already completed to indicate style and period (i.e. Baroque, Classical, or Romantic) • Harmonic analysis may be required

2. Harmony (Keyboard Style)
Continue a keyboard accompaniment for a given solo line (for either voice or instrument) for approximately 8-12 bars in a similar style. The opening portion of the accompaniment will be given to indicate the style. The answer should include • Modulation to any key and return to the tonic • A rhythm and harmony of musical interest, flow, and unity • Harmonic analysis may be required

3. Counterpoint

The candidate may choose

EITHER

To extend a given opening to create a two-part contrapuntal composition of 16-20 bars in length in the style of a Baroque Invention.
• Include points of imitation and show motivic unity
• Include modulations consistent with the period
• Give chordal analysis of implied harmony

OR

TWO fugal subjects will be given.   The candidate will provide an Answer (real or tonal) for each subject. The candidate will then provide a countersubject in invertible counterpoint for either ONE of the subjects.
• Include a modulatory link (or bridge) between the subject and answer, if necessary
• Give chordal analysis of implied harmony

NOTE: A study of the following works (any edition) will assist candidates in preparing for the examination:

Bach, J.S.	*Two-part Inventions*
Bach, J.S.	*Well-Tempered Clavier, Vols. I and II*
Bach, J.S.	*The Art of Fugue*
Riemenschneider, A (ed.)	*371 Harmonized Chorales* (Schirmer)

And also a selection of Lieder representing Schubert, Schumann, Brahms, and Wolf.

FORM & ANALYSIS

(Associate Diploma)

ONE PAPER: **Time: 3 Hours**

RECOMMENDED TEXTS

No one text is complete insofar as these requirements are concerned and, though discrepancies between sources are not unusual, candidates are encouraged to consult a variety of sources. A selective list of theory resource books may be found under the Bibliography section at the end of this syllabus. However, though candidates may choose any text book(s) the following are recommended.

Berry, Wallace, *Form in Music* (Prentice Hall, 1966)

CO-REQUISITE

Successful completion of Theory 7(B) is required to obtain the ASSOCIATE DIPLOMA.

Note: Musical terminology as used in the recommended text is acceptable for examination purposes.

REQUIREMENTS

It is recommended that candidates complete Theory 7(A) before proceeding to Theory 7(B)

Keys required for this examination

Major	ALL keys
Minor	ALL keys

1. Formal Structures
Be familiar with the formal characteristics and historical development of the following forms: • Binary (all types) • Ternary • Rondo • Theme and Variations (including Chaconne & Passacaglia) • Sonata Form • Fugue • Song types (such as strophic, modified-strophic, through-composed, etc.)

2. Analysis
Provide detailed analysis for given musical examples, representing no more than THREE of the above forms, as follows: • Identify key • Trace thematic and motivic development • Mark phrases and cadences • Identify main key centres, points of modulation, key relationships and structural divisions • Harmonic analysis (as requested for selected passages) using chord symbols and figures. Non-harmonic notes to be circled and labelled

HISTORY 5

ONE PAPER:	**Time: 3 Hours**
REQUIRED TEXT	Fortney, Kristine & Machlis, Joseph, **The Enjoyment of Music;** An Introduction to Perceptive Listening. 11th edition. (Norton, 2011)
RECOMMENDED TEXTS	**The Norton Recordings:** Eight Cd's to Accompany the Norton Scores & The Enjoyment of Music. 11th edition (Norton, 2011) Fortney, Kristine (editor), **The Norton Scores:** a Study Anthology. 11th edition (Norton, 2011)
CO-REQUISITE	Successful completion of History 5 OR History 6 is required to obtain a certificate for the Grade 9 Practical Examination.

NOTE: Candidates may complete History 5 and History 6 in the order of their choice.

General Description

History 5 is Part I of a survey of the evolution of musical composition from the Middle Ages to the end of the Classical Period (approximately 1800) with representative composers, compositions, and musical terminology. Candidates should be able to answer questions on the content given below. Not all pieces on the accompanying recordings are required. However, it is important that candidates have a working knowledge of the required compositions listed below, both from their study of the score and from listening to recorded performance.

The selected list of reference and text books given in the Bibliography section at the end of this Syllabus will provide additional sources of information that candidates will find helpful.

Requirements

All requirements, including the score of musical examples, will be found in the required textbook. All required listening examples are taken from the Norton Recordings that accompany the textbook. Nevertheless, candidates are encouraged to listen to other works and also to read articles and other books on the topics required below.

A. Medieval

See *The Enjoyment of Music*, Prelude 2 AND Chapters 12-13

Musical Type/Genre	Terms/Forms/ Styles	Representative Composers	Required Listening
1)Sacred	Plainchant Organum Notre Dame School Modes Neumes Mass (Proper & Ordinary) Motet Isorhythm Ostinato	Hildegard of Bingen Léonin Pérotin	Gregorian Chant: *Kyrie* Hildegard of Bingen: *Alleluia, O Virga mediatrix* Notre Dame School Organum: *Gaude Maria virgo*
2)Secular	Troubadours Trouvères Minnesingers Jongleurs Goliard Songs Courtly poetry	De Vaqueiras Moniot D`Arras	Raimbaut de Vaqueiras: *Kalenda maya*
3)Ars Nova	Polyphonic Mass Isorythmic motet	Machaut	Machaut: *Puis qu'en oubli*
4) Instrumental Music	Soft instruments Loud instruments Organs Improvised music Embellishments		

B. Renaissance   See *The Enjoyment of Music*, Chapters 14-15

Musical Type/Genre	Terms/Forms/ Styles	Representative Composers	Required Listening
1) Sacred	Parts of the Mass Requiem Cantus Firmus Mass Motet Counter-Reformation Council of Trent A cappella	Dufay Josquin Desprez Palestrina	Du Fay: *L'homme armé Mass, Kyrie* Josquin: *Ave Maria...virgo serena* Palestrina: *Pope Marcellus Mass, Gloria*
2) Secular	Burgundian chanson Rondeau Ballade Virelai Pavane Galliard Allemande Ronde	Ockeghem Josquin Desprez Susato	Josquin: *Mille regretz* Susato: *Three Dances*
3) Italian madrigal	Type of texts Performance style & forces	Marenzio Monteverdi Arcadelt	Arcadelt: *Il bianco e dolce cigno*
4) English madrigal	Elizabethan Age	Farmer Wilbye Morley Weelkes	Farmer: *Fair Phyllis*

C. Baroque See *The Enjoyment of Music*, Prelude 3 AND Chapters 16-20

Musical Type/Genre	Terms/Forms/ Styles	Representative Composers	Required Listening
1) General	The Camerata Monody Stile rappresentativo Basso continuo Figured bass Tonality Equal temperament Chromaticism Terraced dynamics		
2) Venetian School	Polychoral music Antiphonal Style St. Mark's Basillica	G. Gabrieli	Gabrieli: *Canzona septimi toni*
3) Opera	Recitative & aria Overture Libretto Ritornello French tragèdie lyrique Opera seria Stile concitato	Monteverdi Purcell Strozzi	Monteverdi: *The Coronation of Poppea,* Act III, Scene 7 Purcell: *Dido and Aeneas,* Act III, Dido's Lament and Chorus Strozzi: *Amor dormiglione (Sleepyhead, Cupid!)*
3) Cantata	Cantata Lutheran Chorale	J.S. Bach	Bach: Cantata No. 140, *Wachet auf,* No. 1, 2, 3, 4, 7.
4) Oratorio	Oratorio French Overture Da capo aria	J.S. Bach Handel	Handel: *Messiah,* Nos. 1, 14, 17, 18, 44
5) Instrumental Music	Baroque instruments Solo concerto Concerto grosso Dance forms & rhythms Church sonatas Chamber sonatas Trio Sonatas Passacaglia & Chaconne Suites Chorale prelude Overtures (French & English) Fugal Form and its devices Prelude & Fugue	D. Scarlatti J.S. Bach Vivaldi Handel	Scarlatti: *Sonata in C major, K. 159 (The Hunt)* Vivaldi: *Spring,* from *The Four Seasons* Handel: *Water Music,* Allegro and Alla hornpipe Bach: *Contrapunctus 1,* from *The Art of Fugue*

D. Classical See *The Enjoyment of Music*, Prelude 4 AND Chapters 21-26

Musical Type/Genre	Terms/Forms/ Styles	Representative Composers	Required Listening
1)General	Rococo Age of Enlightenment Empfindsamkeit Sonata-allegro form Types of movements Exposition Development Recapitulation Coda Absolute Music	Couperin Rameau C.P.E. Bach Gluck	
2) Chamber Music	Divertimento Serenade String Quartet Other Ensembles	Haydn Mozart	Haydn: *String Quartet, Op. 76, No. 3* (2nd mov't) Mozart: *Eine kleine Nachtmusik (A Little Night Music), K. 525* (3rd & 4th mov'ts)
3) Symphony	The classical orchestra Types of movements	Haydn Mozart Beethoven	Mozart: *Symphony No. 40 in G minor* (1st mov't) Beethoven: *Symphony No. 5 in C minor, Op. 67* (1st mov't)
4) Solo Concerto	Types of movements Cadenza	Haydn Mozart Beethoven	Mozart: *Piano Concerto in G major, K. 453* (1st mov't)
5) Sonata	Summary of movements	Haydn Mozart Beethoven	Beethoven: *Piano sonata in C-sharp minor, Op. 27, No 2* (1st mov't)
6) Choral Music	Mass Requiem Oratorio	Haydn Mozart	Haydn: *The Creation*, Part I, closing
7) Opera	Opera séria Opera comique	Mozart	Mozart: *Don Giovanni*, Act 1, Scene 2

Examination Paper

All questions will be based on the required text, scores and recordings, though relevant and accurate information from other sources is also welcome.

The format of the question paper will be as follows:

Type of Questions	Approximate Total Marks
Objective questions (multiple choice & fill-in-the-blanks)	30%
Brief definition of terms, etc., either in paragraph or point form, at the candidate's choice.	30%
General questions requiring short answers of three or four lines in paragraph form	25%
Identification of period, style, genre, etc. from excerpt of the score or recorded excerpt. (The student may be required to identify examples by giving the title of the work and the name of composer.)	15%

The following recordings will help younger students to identify, by sound and timbre, the instruments of the orchestra:

Britten, B   *A Young Persons Guide to the Orchestra*

Saint-Saens, C.   *Carnival of the Animals*

Prokofiev, S.   *Peter and the Wolf*

HISTORY 6

ONE PAPER:	**Time: 3 Hours**
REQUIRED TEXT	Fortney, Kristine & Machlis, Joseph, **The Enjoyment of Music;** *An Introduction to Perceptive Listening.* 11th edition. (Norton, 2011)
RECOMMENDED TEXTS	**The Norton Recordings:** *Eight Cd's to Accompany the Norton Scores & The Enjoyment of Music.* 11th edition (Norton, 2011) Fortney, Kristine (editor), **The Norton Scores:** *a Study Anthology.* 11th edition (Norton, 2011)
CO-REQUISITE	Successful completion of History 5 AND History 6 is required for the Grade 10 Practical Examination.

NOTE: Candidates may complete History 5 and History 6 in the order of their choice.

General Description

A continuation of History 5, this is Part II of a survey of the evolution of musical composition from the beginning of the Romantic Period (approximately 1800) to the late 20th Century, with representative composers, compositions, and musical terminology. Candidates should be able to answer questions on the content given below. Not all pieces on the accompanying recordings are required. However, it is important that candidates have a working knowledge of the required compositions listed below, both from their study of the score and from listening to recorded performance.

The selected list of reference and text book given in the Bibliography section at the end of this Syllabus will provide additional sources of information that candidates will find helpful.

Requirements

All requirements, including the score of musical examples, will be found in the required textbook.   All required listening examples are taken from the Norton Recordings that accompany the textbook. Nevertheless, candidates are encouraged to listen to other works and also to read articles and other books on the topics required below.

A. Romantic   See *The Enjoyment of Music,* Prelude 5 AND Chapters 27-33

Musical Type/Genre	Terms/Forms/ Styles	Representative Composers	Required Listening
1)General	French Revolution Romantic Orchestra Exoticism Expanded forms		
2)Solo Song	German Lied Strophic Modified Strophic Through composed Song Cycle Poets	Brahms Schubert R. Schumann	Schubert: *Elfking (Erlkönig)*
3)Piano Music	Intermezzo Mazurka Waltz Ballad Polonaise Prelude Song Without Words Rhapsody Scherzo	Brahms Chopin Mendelssohn Liszt Schubert C.Schumann R.Schumann	Chopin: Mazurka in B-flat minor, Op. 24, No. 4 Liszt: *The Little Bell (La campanella)*
4)Program Symphony	Idée fixe Program music	Berlioz Liszt	Berlioz: *Symphonie fantastique,* Fourth and Fifth Movements
5)Nationalism		Chopin Dvorak Glinka Smetana Tchaikovsky Borodin Rimsky-Korsakov Grieg Sibelius	Smetana: *The Moldau*
6)Romantic Symphony	Structure of movements	Beethoven Brahms Medelssohn Tchaikovsky	Brahms: Symphony No. 3 in F Major, Third Movement Dvorak: Symphony No. 9 in E minor, *From the New World,* First Movement

7)The Solo Concerto	The solo virtuoso Cadenza	Beethoven Grieg Mendelssohn R.Schumann Tchaikovsky	Mendelssohn: Violin Concerto in E minor, First Movement
8)Choral Music	Mass Requiem Choral Symphony Oratorio Part-Songs	Mendelssohn Verdi Beethoven Brahms	Verdi: Requiem, *Libera me*, excerpt
9)Opera	Grand opera Lyric opera Opéra comique Singspiel Bel canto Endless melody Leitmotif Chromatic harmony Exoticism	Bizet Offenbach Von Weber Leoncavallo Meyerbeer Rossini Verdi Wagner	Verdi: *Rigoletto*, Act III, excerpts Wagner: *Die Walküre* (The Valkyrie), Act III, opening and Finale
10)Exoticism			Bizet: *Carmen*, Act I, Scenes 4 and 5
11)Ballet	History of ballet Diaghilev	Tchaikovsky	Tchaikovsky: *The Nutcracker*, Three Dances

B. Post-Romantic   See *The Enjoyment of Music*, Prelude 6 AND Chapters 33-34

Musical Type/Genre	*Terms/Forms/ Styles*	*Representative Composers*	*Required Listening*
1) Post-Romantic	Symphonies Symphonic Poems Operas	Mahler R. Strauss	Mahler: *The Song of the Earth (Das Led von der Erde)*, Third Movement
2) Impressionism	Impressionist painters Symbolist poets Whole tone scale Parallel chords Harmonic structure Orchestral colour Small forms Programmatic French painters	Debussy Ravel	Debussy: *Prelude to "The Afternoon of a Faun"*
3) Post-Impressionism		Ravel	Ravel: Two Songs from *Don Quixote to Dulcinea*

C. 20th Century to 1950 See *The Enjoyment of Music*, Chapters 35-39

Musical Type/Genre	Terms/Forms/ Styles	Representative Composers	Required Listening
1) Early Century	Dadaism Polyrhythm Polychords Polyharmony Polytonality Atonality Serialism Tone Row	Stravinsky	Stravinsky: *The Rite of Spring*, Part I, excerpts
2) Second Viennese School	Expressionism Sprechstimme Klangfarbenmelodie	Schoenberg Berg Webern	Schoenberg: *Pierrot Lunaire*, Nos. 18 and 21 Berg: *Wozzeck*, Act III, Scene 4, Interlude, and Scene 5
3) Nationalism	Les Six Neo-classicism	Satie Milhaud Bartók Rachmaninoff Elgar Britten Kodaly Poulenc Hindemith Orff Shostakovich R.Strauss Vaughn Williams	Bartòk: *Interrupted Intermezzo,* from *Concerto for Orchestra*
4) American Traditions		Ives Crawford Copland	Ives: *Country Band March* Copland: *Appalachian Spring*, excerpts

D. Music Beyond the Concert Hall   See *The Enjoyment of Music*, Prelude 7 AND
Chapters 40-43

Musical Type, Genre	Terms/Forms/ Styles	Representative Composers	Required Listening
1) Ragtime, Blues, Jazz	Ragtime Blues New Orleans Jazz Scat singing Swing Big Band Bebop Cool Jazz West Coast Jazz Latin Jazz Third Stream Fusion Free jazz New age jazz	Scott Joplin Billie Holiday Duke Ellington Billy Strayhorn Dizzy Gillespie Charlie Parker	Joplin: *Maple Leaf Rag* Strayhorn/Ellington: *Take the A Train* Gillespie/Parker: *A Night in Tunisia*
2) Music Theatre	Operetta Musical	Rodgers and Hammerstein George Gershwin Andrew Lloyd Webber Leonard Bernstein	Bernstein: *West Side Story*, excerpts
3) Music for Films	Underscoring Source music Silent film music Theremin Synthsizer	Max Steiner Bernard Hermann Miklós Rósza Aaron Copland Leonard Bernstein John Williams	
4) Rock Music	Styles and types of early rock music Rock and roll Rockability Motown Rock in the 70s Rock in the 80s Country and Western	Beatles Mick Jagger Bob Dylan	

E. World War II and Beyond See the Enjoyment of Music, Prelude 8 & Chapters 44-47

Musical Type, Genre	Terms/Forms/ Styles	Representative Composers	Required Listening
1) Modern Age	Avant-garde Total serialism Serialism	Olivier Messiaen Pierre Boulez George Crumb	Messiaen: *Quartet for the End of Time*, Second Movement Crumb: *Caballito Negro (Little Black Horse)*
2) World Music	Prepared Piano Javanese gamelan Wayang, sléndro, pélog Metallophones East African music Western and Asian combination Chinese Traditional music	John Cage György Ligeti Bright Sheng Abing	
3) Technology and Music	Music concrete Electronic music MIDI Hyperinstruments Interactivity	Edgar Varèse Milton Babbitt Mario Davidovsky Pauline Oliveras Todd Machover	Machover: *Hyperstring Trilogy: Begin Again, Again …* excerpts
4) Current Trends	Neoromanticism Minimalism Spiritual minimalism Post-minimalism Postmodern Postromanticism Quotation music	Jennifer Higdon John Corigliano Arvo Pärt John Adams	Adams: *Doctor Atomic*, excerpts

Examination Paper

All questions will be based on the required text, scores and recordings, though relevant and accurate information from other sources is also welcome.

The format of the question paper will be as follows:

Type of Questions	Approximate Total Marks
Objective questions (multiple choice & fill-in-the-blanks)	30%
Brief definition of terms, etc., either in paragraph or point form, at the candidate's choice.	30%
General questions requiring short answers of three or four lines in paragraph form	25%
Identification of period, style, genre, etc. from excerpt of the score or recorded excerpt. (The student may be required to identify examples by giving the title of the work and the name of composer.)	15%

HISTORY 7

ONE PAPER:	**Time: 3 Hours**
RECOMMENDED TEXTS	See Recommended texts listed below
PRE-REQUISITES	Candidates must complete both History 5 and History 6 (in any order) before proceeding to History 7
CO-REQUISITE	Successful completion of History 7 is required to obtain the ASSOCIATE DIPLOMA

Requirements

The course is divided into two parts as follows:

Part I   Submission of a brief essay (minimum 2000 words): 20 marks

Part II   A written examination: 80 marks

PART I: Essay on Canadian Music

Candidates will prepare a brief essay on ANY ONE of the topics listed below, to be enclosed at the time of the examination with the completed examination paper. Because this course is a diploma level course, it is assumed that candidates are able to accumulate and organize information on their chosen topic from a number of different sources, and to express themselves clearly in writing. Candidates may use whatever resource material they feel is important. All sources should be properly documented, with footnotes as appropriate and a bibliography.

The essay is to be typewritten on plain white paper, double-spaced, with margins of at least 1 inch. The cover page should include only the candidate's examination number and the title of the essay.

Essays submitted previously to other institutions, for credit or otherwise, may NOT be submitted for this examination.

Essay Topics:

Healey Willan and his influence on the next generations of composers in Canada

The composition of choral music in Canada since 1945

Three leading composers of music for piano in Canada since 1945 *[Three composers to be chosen by the candidate]*

The foundation for new directions in Canadian music for the 21st century *[Discuss the works and influence of ANY TWO composers active in the 1990s]*

Film music by Canadians

The use of indigenous native music in Canadian compositions

R. Murray Schafer: An experimenter

Violet Archer, Jean Coulthard and Barbara Pentland: Ahead of their time?

The stage works of Harry Somers

Three leading Canadian jazz composers since 1945 *[Three composers to be chosen by the candidate]*

Candidates may also submit their own choice of topic to the Registrar for approval. Requests must be made in writing and be received by the Conservatory office at least 30 days before the deadline for application for the examination session.

PART II: Written Examination

Candidates will choose to complete a detailed study of ANY ONE of the following historical periods:

(A) **Renaissance & Baroque**

Recommended Texts:
Freedman, Richard. *Music in the Renaissance* and accompanying anthology. (Norton, 2013)

Heller, Wendy. *Music in the Baroque* and accompanying anthology. (Norton, 2014)

(B) **Classical**

Recommended Text
Downs, Philip G.: *Classical Music: The Era of Haydn, Mozart and Beethoven* and accompanying anthology (Norton, 1991)

(C) **Romantic & Impressionist**

Recommended Text
Frisch, Walter.: *Music in the Nineteenth Century* and accompanying anthology. (Norton, 2013)

(D) **20ᵗʰ and 21ˢᵗ Century**

Recommended Text
Auner, Joseph. *Music in the Twentieth and Twenty-First Centuries* and accompanying anthology. (Norton, 2013)

(E) **Canadian Music**

Recommended Text
Keillor, Elaine. *Music in Canada: Capturing Landscape and Diversity*. (McGill-Queen's University Press, 2006)

Candidates should concentrate of historical chronology, leading composers and their influence, musical examples, and the development of styles, forms and compositional techniques. *Candidates are expected to support their answers with appropriate musical examples.* Choose ANY FOUR works (each differing in composer and genre) that you consider representative of the period you are studying and through the study of scores and recordings, be prepared to discuss and refer to them in the written examination.

The selective list of reference and text books given in the Bibliography section at the end of this Syllabus will provide additional sources of information that candidates will find helpful.

Examination Paper

All questions will be based on information contained in standard written sources for the period chosen, and also on musical scores and recordings of typical examples.

Marks for History 7 will be divided as follows:

Type of Questions	Total Marks
PART II (Examination Paper) General questions requiring short answer of three or four lines in paragraph form. Some choice will be given.	30
One essay-type question on the chosen works	25
One general essay-type question on the period	25
TOTAL MARKS FOR PART II (EXAMINATION PAPER)	80
TOTAL MARKS FOR PART I (ESSAY)	20

BIBLIOGRAPHY

The following books are useful for study reference and teaching purposes:

DICTIONARIES AND ENCYCLOPEDIAS

Arnold, D. ed. *The New Oxford Companion to Music* (Oxford University Press, 1983)
Kallman, H, Potvin, G. & Winters, K., eds. *Encyclopedia of Music in Canada* (U of T Press, 1992)
Kernfeld, B. ed. *The New Grove Dictionary of Jazz* (Oxford University Press, 2002)
Latham, A. ed. *The Oxford Companion to Music* (Oxford University Press, 2003)
Randel, D.M. ed. *New Harvard Dictionary of Music* (Harvard University Press, 2002)
Read, G. *Music Notation; a Manual of Modern Practice.* 2nd edition. (Parkwest, 1979)
Sadie, S. & Tyrell, J. eds. *The New Grove Dictionary of Music and Musicians:* 29 volumes with index. (Oxford University Press, 2004)
Sadie, S. ed. *The New Grove Dictionary of Opera:* 4 volumes (Oxford University Press, 2004)
Slonimsky, N. & Kuhn, L.D. eds. *Baker's Biographical Dictionary of Musicians* (Schirmer, 2002)
Warrack, J.H. & West, E., eds. *The Concise Oxford Dictionary of Opera* (Oxford University Press, 1992)

ANTHOLOGIES

Burkhart, C. & Rothstein, W., eds. *Anthology for Musical Analysis.* 7th edition. (Schirmer, 2011)
Burkholder, J.P. & Palisca, C.V., eds. *The Norton Anthology of Western Music* (Norton, 2009)
Downs, P. *Anthology of Classical Music* (Norton, 1992)
Forney, K. ed. *The Norton Scores: A Study Anthology* (Norton, 2011)
Hoppin, R.H. *An Anthology of Medieval Music* (Norton, 1978)
Kostka, S. & Graybill, R. *An Anthology of Music for Analysis* (Pearson, 2003
Riemenschneider, A. ed. *371 Harmonized Chorales and 69 Chorale Melodies with Figured Bass by Johann Sebastian Bach* (Schirmer, 1941)
Wennerstrom, M. ed. *Anthology of Twentieth Century Music.* 2nd edition. (Pearson, 1987)

BOOKS

Harmony and Counterpoint

Aldwell, E., Schachter, C., & Cadwallader, A. *Harmony & Voice Leading.* 4th edition. (Schirmer, 2010)
---workbooks, Vol. 1 and Vol. 2Muis
Andrews, W.G. & Sclater, M. *Elements of 18th Century Counterpoint* (Alfred, 1997)
Andrews, W.G. & Sclater, M. *Materials of Western Music.* Parts I – III (Alfred, 1997)
Benjamin, T. *Counterpoint in the Style of J.S. Bach* (Schirmer, 1986)
Gauldin, R. *Harmonic Practice in Tonal Music* 2nd Edition (Norton, 2004)
Kennan, K.W. *Counterpoint: Based on 18th Century Practice* (Pearson, 1998)

Kennan, K.W. *Workbook for Counterpoint Based on 18th Century Practice* (Pearson, 1998)
Laitz, S.G. *The Complete Musician.* 3d edition (Oxford University Press, 2011)
Laitz, S.G. *Writing and Analysis Workbook to Accompany the Complete Musician.* Oxford University Press, 2011)
Mason, N.B. *The Essentials of Eighteenth-Century Counterpoint* (W.C.Brown, 1978)
Piston, W., Jannery, A. & DeVoto, M. *Harmony* (Norton, 1987)
Piston, W. *Workbook for Harmony.* 5th edition (Norton, 1987)
Ottman, R.W. *Advanced Harmony: Theory and Practice* 5th edition (Pearson, 2000)
Ottman, R.W. *Elementary Harmony: Theory and Practice* 5th edition (Pearson, 1997)

Form and Analysis

Berry, Wallace *Form in Music* (Prentice Hall, 1966)
Green, D. M. *Form in Tonal Music.* 2nd Edition (Schirmer, 1979)
Iliffe, F. *Bach's 48 Preludes and Fugues Analysed for Students.* 2 volumes (Hal Leonard, 2010)
MacPherson, S. *Form in Music* (Pomona Press, 2008) (also Kindle)
Rosen, H. *Sonata Forms (*Norton, 1985)
Stein, L. *Structure and Style* (Kindle Edition only)
Tovey, D.F. *A Companion to the Beethoven Pianoforte Sonatas* (ABRSM, 1999)

Music History

General

Abraham, G. *The Concise Oxford History of Music* (Oxford University Press, 1980)
Bonds, Mark Evans. *A History of Music in Western Culture.* 4th ed. (Pearson, 2013)
Burkholder, J. Peter, Donald Jay Grout and Claude V. Palisca *A History of Western Music.* 9th ed. (Norton, 2014) Accompanying Anthology and CDs
Hanning, Barbara *Concise History of Western Music.* 5th ed. (Norton, 2014)
Lopinski, J., Ringhofer, J.,& Zarins, P. *Explorations, Explorations 2, Explorations 3* (Frederick Harris, 2010)
Machlis, Joseph and Kristine Forney. *The Enjoyment of Music.* 11ed. (Norton, 2011)

Renaissance & Baroque

Atlas, Alan W. *Renaissance Music: Music in Western Europe 1400 – 1600* and accompanying anthology. *(*Norton, 1998)
Anthony, J. et al *The New Grove French Baroque Masters* (Norton, 1987)
Arnold, D. *The New Grove Italian Baroque Masters* (Norton, 1997)
Brown, Howard Mayer *Music in the Renaissance.* (Prentice Hall, 1999)
Freedman, Richard. *Music in the Renaissance* and accompanying anthology. (Norton, 2013)
Heller, Wendy. *Music in the Baroque* and accompanying anthology. (Norton, 2014)
Hoppin, R.H. *Medieval Music* (Norton, 1978)
Noble, J. , & Reese *The New Grove High Renaissance Masters (Norton, 1984)*
Palisca, Claude V.   *Baroque Music.* 3rd ed. (Prentice Hall, 1991)
Schulenberg, David *Music of the Baroque* and accompanying anthology. 3rd ed. (Oxford University Press, 2013)
Seay, A. *Music in the Medieval World* (Waveland Press, 1991)
Yudkin, J. *Music in Medieval Europe* (Pearson, 1989)

Classical

Downs, Philip G.   *Classical Music: The Era of Haydn, Mozart and Beethoven* and accompanying anthology. (Norton, 1991)
Pauly, Reinhard G.   *Music in the Classical Period.* (Prentice Hall, 1999)
Rosen, Charles   *The Classical Style: Haydn, Mozart, Beethoven.* (Norton, 1998)

Romantic

Finson, Jon W.   *Nineteenth-Century Music: The Western Classical Tradition.* (Prentice Hall, 2002)
Frisch, Walter   *Music in the Nineteenth Century* and accompanying anthology. (Norton, 2013)
Plantinga, Leon   *Romantic Music.* (Norton, 1985)
Rosen, Charles   *The Romantic Generation.* 5th edition. (Harvard University Press, 1998)

Twentieth Century

Auner, Joseph *Music in the Twentieth and Twenty-First Centuries* and accompanying anthology. (Norton, 2013)
Austin, Larry, Douglas Kahn and Nilendra Gurusinghe, editors.   *Source: Music of the Avant-garde, 1966-1973* (University of California Press, 2011)
Cope, David   *New Directions in Music.* 7th edition. (Waveland Press, 2000)
Salzman, Eric   *Twentieth-Century Music: An Introduction.* (Prentice Hall, 2001)
Sitsky, Larry   *Music of the Avant-Garde: A Biocritical Sourcebook.* (Greenwood, 2002)

Canadian Music

Keillor, Elaine *Music in Canada: Capturing Landscape and Diversity*. (McGill-Queen's University Press, 2006)
McGee, Timothy   *Music in Canada.* (Norton, 1985)

NOTES

NOTES